I LOVE YOU
WITH ALL MY
HEART

Farabee Publishing | Chandler, AZ 85224

ISBN: 979-8-89034-074-0

Printed in the United States of America

Designed by: Vinesh Kumar J

I LOVE YOU WITH ALL MY HEART

Dedicated to Zaiden C. Moore

You are and always will be my best best buddy. You are so special to me.

Since the day you were born, you have taught me so much about life and more. Never stop being you.

I love you with all my heart.

Love Always and Forever,

Daddy.

The day you were born was a brand new start.
A dad I now am,
I love you with all my heart!

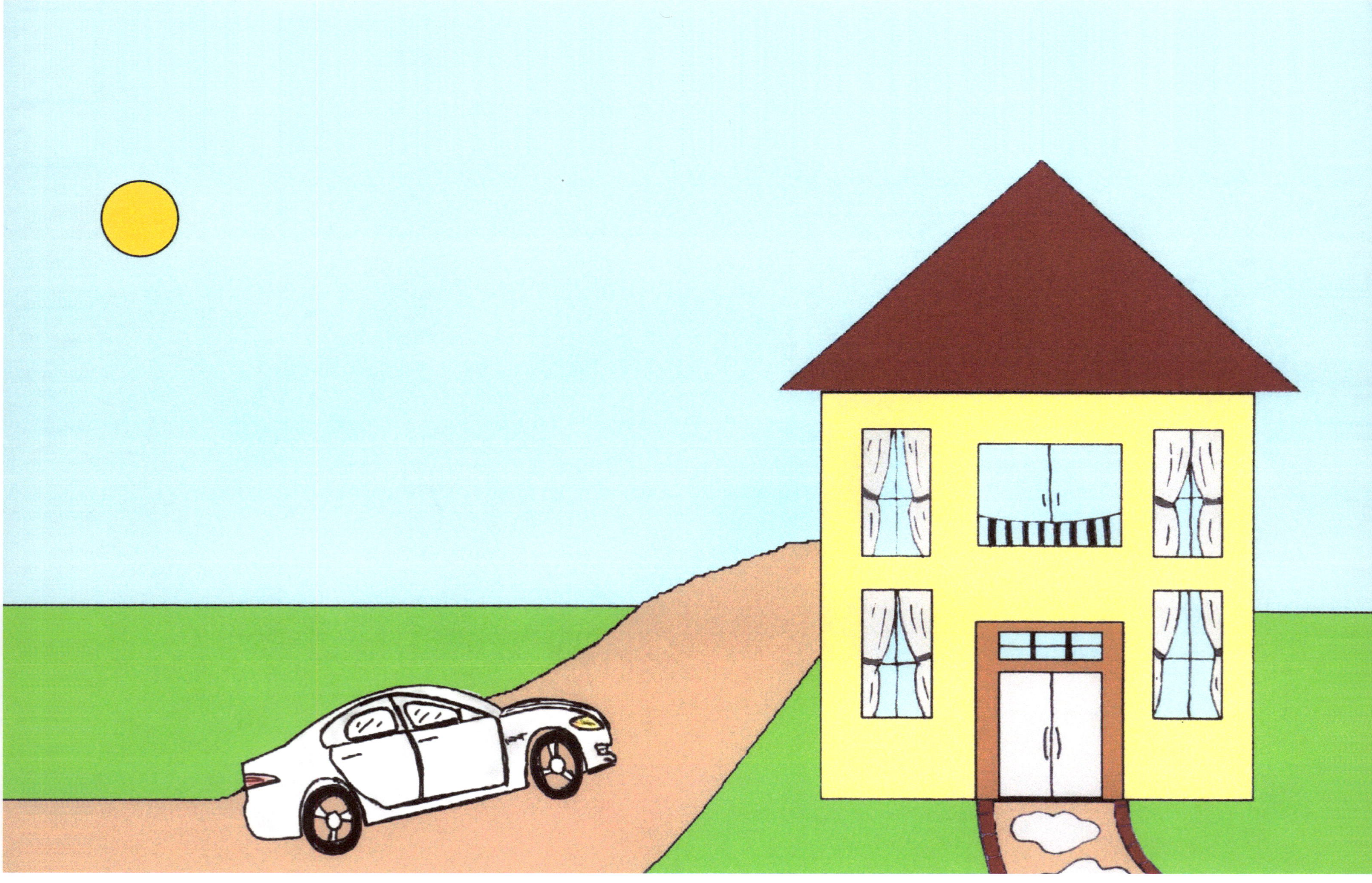

So tiny you are, we bring you home for a brand new start.
I love you with all my heart!

Everyday goes by and you grow more and more.
Every second just know,
I love you with all my heart!

You are so special and so smart.
Every day is a delight when I'm with you.
I love you with all my heart!

You're always so polite and never ever rude.
You're such a caring kid and you make me so proud.
I love you with all my heart!

Every night I tuck you in, comfy and warm.
Wishing you the sweetest dreams.
I love you with all my heart!

From the time I wake up and until I go to bed,
I'm always thinking of you.
I love you with all my heart!

We plant gardens together and run through the dirt.
Every minute with you is a treasure that I'll never forget.
I love you with all my heart!

So many adventures and millions of memories made.
Every second I'm with you, my day is so bright.
I love you with all my heart!

We do have our struggles, but that's part of growing up. I'm always here for you no matter what.
I love you with all my heart!

Every day I teach you new things and I'd be silly not to say,
you teach me new things too, every single day!
I love you with all my heart!

As you keep growing, keep shooting for the stars! One day they will all be in your arms.
I love you with all my heart!

Your future is so bright and the world has much to offer,
but you have so much more to offer the world.
I love you with all my heart!

Your smile could light up a room and brighten anyone's day,
I look forward to seeing it each time you awake.
I love you with all my heart!

Anytime I'm away, I miss you so, so much. You're my best, best buddy!
I love you with all my heart!

You're such a great kid, so amazing and smart. Never stop growing and learning.

Most importantly, never stop being YOU! I love you with all my heart!